Unseen > seen

Unseen > seen
Copyright © 2025 by Isabel Mireya Tufano

Published by 3 Point Turn Publishing
Brea, CA
www.3pointturn.org

ISBN: 979-8-9941140-0-1

First Edition
Unless otherwise indicated, all Scripture quotations are taken from the Holy Bible, New Living Translation (**NLT**). Copyright © 1996, 2004, 2015 by Tyndale House Foundation. Used by permission. All rights reserved.

Scripture quotations marked **NIV** are from the Holy Bible, New International Version®. Copyright © 1973, 1978, 1984, 2011 by Biblica, Inc.™ Used by permission. All rights reserved worldwide.

Scripture quotations marked **NKJV** are from the New King James Version®. Copyright © 1982 by Thomas Nelson. Used by permission. All rights reserved.

Unseen > seen

"How obedient faith can save your family"

Isabel Mireya Tufano

Table of Contents

Dedication

This book is dedicated to my husband—Joshua Tufano—who has always been my biggest fan. Thank you for being my Dwayne and always exhorting me to go higher and higher with Jesus!

"And we know that all things work together for good to those who love God, to those who are the called according to His purpose." Romans 8:28 (NKJV)

To my mom—thank you for leading me to Jesus. Because you planted seeds of faith and pointed me toward the Savior, I found the only path worth walking. That path led to healing, purpose, and ultimately, to the writing of this book. This work is fruit from the tree you helped nurture. I love you, and I'm forever grateful.

HERE'S WHAT PEOPLE ARE SAYING ABOUT
Unseen › seen

"There are few things that are of greater value for a believer than to learn how to target their faith in an area of their life where they're desiring to see God move. Mireya thoroughly delves into some of the most pertinent instances in scripture where someone puts the Word of God to work until they see their family and lineage changed. Let this book stir up your spirit and pure minds to see clearly that when faith gets involved, God gets involved. And when God gets involved, nothing remains impossible."

-Michael Weber
Senior Pastor of Truth & Triumph Christian Assembly
Redlands, CA

"This book is true to God's word and calls us to live from a place of faith, walking in His word. Unseen > seen shows us that the stories in the Bible do not just tell us who God was, but rather who He is to us today. If you apply the things highlighted in this book that are direct from God's word, your life will be changed!"

-Chris Battenschlag
Senior Pastor of Rooted Harvest Church &
CEO of Rooted Harvest Academy
Wildomar, CA

"Unseen > seen is not only a powerful journey through the Bible that reveals how faith in the Unseen shaped history, but a faithfilled walk with biblical heros who trusted Gods promise over their realities. This book provides a compelling look at how obedience to the Unseen changed the course of generations."

-Believer Mike

"God clearly used Mireya Tufano in a powerful way to bring these scriptural examples together into one impactful, yet easy-to-read book. It's rich with truth, accessible to anyone hungry for more of God, and a great resource for deepening your walk of faith. It is a faith-building tool and I am grateful I read it.

-Steven Sedory
Senior Pastor of The Body Church & Owner
of Vertical IT Solutions
Chino, CA

Introduction

The things we see with our eyes are all temporary. It is the Unseen the things of faith in Jesus that are eternal. As believers who have been "born again," we cannot physically see our salvation, yet by faith, we trust that a divine exchange has taken place. Without seeing, we believe we have been transformed from death to life, from sinner to saved. Moreover, as we cling to that faith, visible changes begin to manifest in our lives and in the lives of those around us.

The Bible says that **faith without works is dead:**

James 2:17(NLT) *"So you see, faith by itself isn't enough. Unless it produces good deeds, it is dead and useless."*

Faith begins as an internal transformation but inevitably manifests outwardly. A clear example is a drug addict who receives salvation through Jesus Christ and immediately stops using drugs. The change first occurred in the **Unseen,** but its fruit became evident in the seen. This is the manifestation of a new life in Christ.

2 Corinthians 5:17(NLT) *"Anyone who belongs to Christ has become a new person. The old life is gone; a new life has begun!"*

As we walk in faith, everything about us begins to change our words, our actions, even our desires.

Faith is the key to everything Jesus accomplished through His death and resurrection. Healing, provision, salvation, and transformation all come by faith, and the evidence can be seen in our lives. However, if our faith is just words, is it really faith?

James 2:14(MSG) *"Isn't it obvious that God-talk without God-acts is outrageous nonsense?"*

In other words, **stop just talking about faith start living it!** **2 Corinthians 5:7** doesn't say we are to "speak" by faith; it says we are to **walk** by faith. We are called not only to proclaim God's Word but also to act on it. Faith should be in both our words and our actions. Faith is not only a noun it is also a verb. Faith requires corresponding action.

2 Corinthians 5:7(NKJV) *"For we walk by faith, not by sight."*

The verse above is often quoted by believers and even printed on shirts and blankets, yet many who display it still let circumstances dictate their faith. They speak words of lack, fear, and doubt complaining about the cost of living, worrying about finances, and dwelling on sickness. **That is the opposite of walking by faith. That is walking by sight**.

We are called to speak what the Bible says not what we see or feel in the natural. Faith says stop looking at the natural and start looking at the supernatural. This becomes easy when we read and believe God's Word. If we truly accept, what Scripture says about who we are and what we have in Christ, our faith will produce lasting fruit.

John 15:16(NLT) *"You didn't choose me. I chose you. I appointed you to go and produce lasting fruit, so that the Father will give you whatever you ask for, using my name."*

This fruit includes healing, provision, spiritual maturity, and so much more. God's promises are not conditional on circumstances; they are conditional on faith.

2 Corinthians 1:20(NLT) *"For all of God's promises have been fulfilled in Christ with a* *resounding "Yes!" And through Christ, our "Amen" ascends to God for his glory."*

If our words do not align with the Bible, then faith is not truly in our hearts.

Luke 6:45(NLT) *"What you say flows from what is in your heart."*

Just as good fruit comes from a healthy tree, our words and actions are evidence of the faith within us. If the tree dies, the fruit dies with it.

Throughout Scripture, we see faith unlocking miracles:

Luke 8:48(NLT), 18:42(NLT) *"Your faith has made you well."*

Acts 3:16(NLT) *"Through faith in the name of Jesus, this man was healed and you know how crippled he was before. Faith in Jesus' name has healed him before your very eyes."*

Miracles happen only through faith in Jesus. Nevertheless, faith must extend beyond salvation it must be the foundation of our daily lives. Many believe God can heal and provide, but do they believe He will? That gap between knowing what God can do and trusting what He will do is **unbelief.**

Hebrews 11:3(MSG) *"What we see was created by what we can't see."*

If you ask a believer who created the world, they will confidently say, God did. Yet, no one saw Him do it. So why do some limit their faith? Why trust God for creation and salvation, but not for healing and provision? The root issue is not a lack of faith it is **unbelief**.

Look at Thomas:

John 20:25(NLT) *"They told him, "We have seen the Lord!" But he replied, "I won't believe it unless I see the nail wounds in His hands, put my fingers into them, and place my hand into the wound in His side."*

Thomas refused to believe without seeing. We all know believers like that maybe we have been one of them. Many give up before they see their faith come to pass and die in the wilderness without ever entering the Promised Land. Worse, unbelief is contagious, and instead of a testimony of faith, it becomes a testimony of failure.

Thank God, for biblical examples of unwavering faith like **Abraham**, **Joseph**, and **David**, who refused to give up.

So the question is: **Are we following signs and wonders, or are we following Jesus?**

Shadrach, Meshach, and Abednego followed God despite the cost. That's why they boldly declared:

Daniel 3:17-18(NLT) *"If we are thrown into the blazing furnace, the God whom we serve is able to save us. But even if He doesn't, we will never serve your gods."*

Like the woman with the issue of blood, you may not know how God will do it, but faith tells you that if you can just **touch the hem of His garment**, you will receive that for which you believe.

Faith moves mountains, but **trust** brings the desires of our hearts. Trust is what unfolds God's plan for our lives.

Proverbs 3:5-6(NLT) *"Trust in the Lord with all your heart; do not depend on your own understanding. Seek His will in all you do, and He will show you which path to take."*

Many believers can quote this verse, but how many actually let God direct their steps?

During COVID, we didn't see many believers walking in faith and trusting God did we? **Psalm**

37:3-5(NKJV) says that trusting in God produces supernatural movement on our behalf. If we are not experiencing that, it is time to examine where our trust truly lies.

The Bible is full of stories of men and women who looked beyond the natural into the supernatural and by faith, received what they believed for. Their obedient faith saved not only themselves but their families as well.

The question is: **Will we be among them?**

Chapter 1: Abraham

Faith That Saves Your Family Requires Sacrifice

Faith that can save your family requires the sacrifice of who and what you love most **(Genesis 22:1-2 NLT, 12:1-3 NLT, Matthew 10:39 NLT)**.

God told Abraham, "Take your son, whom you love so much, and sacrifice him on the altar." This command reveals a profound truth: our love for anyone or anything above the **Unseen** God must be surrendered in order to see our families saved. Like Abraham, we must be willing to lose them in the natural to gain them for the Kingdom of God.

The story of Abraham's faith is one of sacrifice leading to supernatural gain. Before we pity him for what he was asked to give up, we must recognize that what he gained was far greater. His harvest far exceeded the seeds he sowed. What seemed like a loss was returned to him in abundance. Where God required the sacrifice of one son, He made Abraham the father of an innumerable lineage. His bloodline extends throughout time, making him our father in the faith. The sacrifice of one produced countless many; that is the blessing of multiplication that comes from faith in the **Unseen** God.

Abraham's life stands as a banner proclaiming that the **Unseen is greater than the seen**. He paved the way for the world to walk in faith and receive the promises of God. Through him came David, and through David came Jesus the **Unseen God made manifest in the seen (John 1:14 NLT)**.

A Journey of Faith and Obedience

God called Abraham to co-labor with Him in faith, asking him to leave everything and everyone he knew to follow an **Unseen** plan that would take decades to unfold. Yet, Abraham believed God at His word and obeyed, despite having no tangible evidence of what was to come. Thousands of years later, we continue to reap the benefits of the covenant established through his faith and obedience.

With every step forward in faith, Abraham was required to sacrifice more. The greatest test came when God asked for Isaac the long-awaited, promised son. Abraham had patiently endured years of waiting, but his trust in God had forged an intimate relationship. The Bible tells us that upon receiving God's command, **he rose early the next morning** and set out for the place God had shown him. There was no hesitation. Such immediate obedience only comes from a life steeped in faith and trust in the **Unseen** God.

Abraham knew God. He knew His character, His faithfulness, and His love. He had already experienced God as a **promise-keeper**. Since God had said that Abraham's descendants would come through Isaac, he trusted that somehow, God would fulfill His word even if it meant raising Isaac from the dead **(Hebrews 11:19 NLT)**.

Do We Trust Like Abraham?

We should ask ourselves:

- Do we believe in God's promise-keeping character like Abraham did?
- Do we truly trust that the **Unseen** is greater than the seen?
- Do we have such an intimate relationship with God that we can move forward in faith, sacrificing without hesitation?

Abraham was able to see beyond the natural into the supernatural. As children of God, we are called to do the same. If we live by what we can see, taste, touch, and experience alone, we risk becoming carnal Christians governed by the flesh rather than by faith. In addition, **when we cannot see beyond the flesh, the flesh has already won.**

The Bible is clear: *"For we walk by faith, not by sight"* **(2 Corinthians 5:7 NKJV)**. And *"Without* *faith, it is impossible to please God"* **(Hebrews 11:6 NKJV).**

We must choose to believe God at His word, just as our father Abraham did. Our faith today will impact the generations that come after us.

Do you love your family enough to trust God completely?

Because **He does**.

Chapter 2: Noah

Faith That Stands Alone

The Bible describes Noah as a just man, perfect in his generation **(Genesis 6:9 NLT)**. He wasn't simply the most righteous man in his town or his country he was the **only** righteous man on the **entire** earth. Imagine that. In a world completely corrupted by sin and violence, Noah stood alone in faith and obedience to God.

Many believers today feel isolated in their faith, as if they are on an island by themselves. However, unlike us, Noah truly was. He did not blend in with the culture around him. He did not conform to the wickedness of his time. Instead, he obeyed the **Unseen** God, walking in faith without fear even when standing out may have proven to be dangerous.

Genesis 6:11 describes the world of Noah's day as **corrupt and filled with violence**. Does that sound familiar? Just as God saw the depth of depravity then, He sees it now.

1 John 4:4(NKJV) *"You are of God, little children, and have overcome them, because He who is in you is greater than he who is in the world."*

Yet, despite humanity's rebellion, His love remains unchanged.

Even amid the darkness, God's love and mercy endures. *"Oh, give thanks to the God of heaven! For His mercy endures forever."* **(Psalm 136:26 NKJV).** His mercy is what restrains His judgment.

2 Peter 3:9(NLT) reminds us: *"The Lord isn't really being slow about His promise, as some people think. No, He is being patient for your sake. He does not want anyone to be destroyed but wants everyone to repent."*

Noah's Exclusive Revelation

Because of Noah's righteousness, he was the only person on earth to whom God revealed His plan:

Genesis 6:13(NLT) *"So God said to Noah, 'I have decided to destroy all living creatures, for they have filled the earth with violence. Yes, I will wipe them all out along with the earth."*

Take a moment to imagine knowing something so crucial something no one else was privy to. Now imagine warning people about it, only to be ridiculed, ignored, and likely hated. If God had spoken to even one other person, perhaps Noah's message would have been easier to believe.

However, that wasn't the case. Noah alone had to trust in the Unseen God and prepare for an **unseen** disaster.

We often view biblical figures like Noah as ordinary people, but the truth is, they were **extraordinary** not because of their own strength, but because of their faith. Noah's life is a powerful picture of what it means to fight the good fight of faith **(1 Timothy 6:12 NKJV)**. He held onto a truth given only to him, making it unbelievable to everyone else.

The Covenant That Saved a Family

Noah's righteousness didn't just earn him divine revelation it also secured a covenant that saved him and his family.

Genesis 6:18(NKJV) *"But I will establish My covenant with you; and you shall go into the ark you, your sons, your wife, and your sons' wives with you."*

The **Unseen** saved the seen. This foreshadows salvation through Jesus Christ. We have never seen Jesus physically, yet He has saved us from **sin, death, and hell**.

The covenant God made with Noah was one of **salvation, not destruction** just as the new covenant through Christ offers eternal life instead of judgment. Now **that** is good news!

A 100-Year Test of Faith

Noah was given a task that took **100 years** to complete an assignment for a future event no one had ever seen before. Yet, he remained **faithful**.

How many believers today abandon their calling at the first sign of difficulty? Noah's story reminds us that obedience to God always produces a reward. The entire world was destroyed, yet Noah and his family were spared.

1 Peter 3:20(NLT) *"Those who disobeyed God long ago when God waited patiently while Noah was building his boat. Only eight people were saved from drowning in that terrible flood."*

The blessing of Noah's obedience should encourage us to remain steadfast in our faith. **Do not allow discouragement to take you off course.** The same unwavering faith Noah displayed is available to all who choose to believe and obey the Lord.

Make sure you are one of those people.

Chapter 3: Joseph

Faith in the Unseen

Joseph, the son of Jacob, had eleven brothers, yet he was undeniably his father's favorite. *"Jacob loved Joseph more than any of his other children because Joseph had been born to him in his old age."* **Genesis 37:3(NLT)**

Joseph never asked to be favored, but the timing of his birth set him apart. This favoritism marked his life and created deep resentment among his brothers, who could not even speak a kind word to him.

To make matters worse, Joseph received two prophetic dreams in which his family, including his brothers and parents, would bow before him. When he shared these dreams, it seemed to confirm that not only was he their father's favorite, but also God's favorite. Their jealousy turned into hatred.

Even **family** can turn against you when you start walking in the calling God has placed on your life.

Joseph's brothers failed to see past the seen into the **Unseen**. Their bitterness blinded them to Joseph's divine destiny one that would later save them from a famine. When we fail to deal with jealousy and resentment, we risk being consumed by them.

This is exactly what happened in the hearts of Joseph's brothers:

Genesis 37:18-20(NLT) *"When Joseph's brothers saw him coming, they recognized him in the distance. As he approached, they made plans to kill him. 'Here comes the dreamer!' they said. 'Come on, let's kill him and throw him into one of these cisterns. We can tell our father, "A wild animal has eaten him." Then we'll see what becomes of his dreams!"*

Joseph's own brothers saw him from a distance and immediately thought of **murder**. The very ones he trusted, plotted to destroy him. This is the enemy's plan to **steal, kill, and destroy (John 10:10 NKJV)**. We all have a choice regarding whom we will serve, and our choices affect not just us, but those around us.

This is why Scripture warns us:

Proverbs 4:23(NLT) *"Guard your heart above all else, for it determines the course of your life."*

Joseph's brothers ultimately decided **not** to kill him but instead sold him to Midianite traders, who then sold him to Potiphar, the captain of Pharaoh's guard. Even in slavery, Joseph remained faithful to God and God remained faithful to him.

Faith Brings Promotion

Joseph's unwavering faith led to undeniable **favor**. Even Potiphar recognized God's hand upon him, promoting Joseph to his personal attendant and putting him in charge of his entire household. This is what happens when we focus on the **Unseen** rather than the seen.

However, **promotion sometimes comes with testing**. For Joseph, the test came through **Potiphar's wife**, who relentlessly pursued him. She was a tool of the enemy, trying to shift Joseph's eyes onto the seen.

The Bible warns us to be *"wise as serpents and harmless as doves"* **(Matthew 10:16 NKJV)**, and Joseph embodied this wisdom. He refused to compromise, yet Potiphar's wife falsely accused him:

Genesis 39:17-18(NLT) *"That Hebrew slave you've brought into our house tried to come in and fool around with me," she said. "But when I screamed, he ran outside, leaving his cloak with me!"*

False accusations began flying around **because Joseph pursued the Unseen**. This led to his unjust imprisonment, yet **God's favor followed him even into the depths of prison**.

Genesis 39:23(NLT) *"The warden had no more worries, because Joseph took care of everything. The LORD was with him and caused everything he did to succeed."*

Joseph's faith never wavered. Instead of dwelling on his circumstances, he remained faithful in every season. While in prison, he correctly interpreted the dreams of Pharaoh's chief cupbearer and chief baker. He asked the cupbearer to remember him when he was restored to Pharaoh's household but **two more years passed in silence**.

At this point, many believers would have given up. We tend to shift our focus to **what we see** our suffering, setbacks, and disappointments. But **not Joseph**. He **never took his eyes off the Unseen**.

Faith That Moves Mountains

Then, at the appointed time, Joseph's breakthrough came. Pharaoh had two troubling dreams that no one could interpret. Suddenly, the chief cupbearer remembered Joseph and spoke of his ability to interpret dreams.

Joseph was immediately summoned before Pharaoh. **Now faith is!**

Not only did Joseph interpret Pharaoh's dreams correctly, but he also presented a God-given plan to save Egypt from the coming famine:

Genesis 41:33-36(NLT) *"Therefore, Pharaoh should find an intelligent and wise man and put him in charge of the entire land of Egypt. Then Pharaoh should appoint supervisors over the land and let them collect one-fifth of all the crops during the* *seven good years. Have them gather all the food produced in the good years that are just ahead and bring it to Pharaoh's storehouses. Store it away, and guard it so there will be food in the cities. That way there will be enough to eat when the seven years of famine come to the land of Egypt. Otherwise, this famine will destroy the land."*

Joseph **walked straight into his destiny**, becoming **second in command over all of Egypt**.

The **Unseen lifted him from the prison to the palace in an instant**.

That is the power of God!

The Fulfillment of the Unseen

Joseph was only thirty years old when his dreams became reality.

The seven years of abundance passed, and famine struck the land. Because of the plan God gave Joseph, Egypt became the only place with food. When Jacob heard that grain was available in Egypt, he sent **ten of his sons** to buy food.

Unbeknownst to them, the man in charge of distributing the grain was **Joseph**. As they bowed before him, **his prophetic dreams were fulfilled (Genesis 42:6 NLT)**. The very thing his brothers hated him for, came to pass.

Joseph recognized his brothers, but they did not recognize him. After testing their hearts to see if they had changed, he finally revealed his identity. His family was **saved** because of his faithfulness to the **Unseen**.

Joseph saw God's hand in every situation whether in his coat of many colors, the pit, slavery, or prison. His story powerfully demonstrates how unwavering faith can save not only us but also our families. God elevated Joseph **not just for his own sake, but for the preservation of his families lineage**.

Genesis 50:20(NLT) *"What the enemy meant for evil, God used to save Joseph's family!"*

Nothing is too hard for God. Keep your eyes on the **Unseen**, and watch His promises unfold.

Chapter 4: Rahab

Rahab was a prostitute in the city of Jericho who took in and hid two Israelite spies sent by the prophet Joshua. God had planned to destroy the city and everyone in it because of their wickedness. When the king of Jericho discovered the spies were staying at Rahab's home, he sent word for her to turn them in.

In the seen realm, Rahab was a prostitute, and her king had given her direct orders regarding these two men she had just met. Normally, obeying would be a no-brainer turn them in and save herself from the wrath of a king who likely held little regard for her. However, something in the **Unseen** moved her to do the opposite. Instead of complying, she hid the spies and went even further, sending the king's men in the wrong direction to chase after them.

Why did this Unseen boldness come upon her?

Joshua 2:9 tells us that Rahab **knew** the land she lived in had been given to the Israelites by their God. She informed the two men that everyone in the city was terrified because of the stories of their God moving on their behalf stories like the miraculous parting of the Red Sea. These testimonies of what had manifested in the seen realm caused her to fear the **Unseen** power of God more than the earthly power of her own king. That was not earthly wisdom; it was wisdom from the Lord.

This **Godly wisdom** gave her the discernment to see that if she had handed the spies over to the king; their God would have destroyed Jericho including her and her family. Instead, she boldly created a covenant with the spies to save herself and her loved ones. She asked the men to return her lifesaving favor by remembering her and her family when they conquered the city **(Joshua 2:12 NLT)**.

The men agreed to the covenant and gave her specific instructions: leave a scarlet rope hanging from her window and make sure all her family members were inside her house (Joshua 2:18 NLT).

Notice that her **faith required corresponding action**. It was not enough to simply believe that God would save her and her family; she had to **co-labor** with Him. She had to follow through hanging the scarlet rope and ensuring her family remained inside. **God always calls us to co-labor with Him to receive the promises He has made to us.** As **James 2:17(NLT)** says, *"Faith without works is dead."*

Just like Rahab, we have a role to play not only in the destiny of our own lives but also in the lives of those we love. Our choices, whether for God or against Him, affect future generations. Any of Rahab's family members who ignored her instructions would have perished with the rest of the city.

Too many of us claim to be **waiting on God** while remaining in disobedience and complacency, doing nothing. Afraid of making the wrong moves, we allow a spirit of fear to paralyze us, keeping us from making any moves at all. That turns us into people who are all talk and no walk people who claimed to miss church when it was closed, rarely attend now that it is open.

James 2:17(AMPC) tells us that a faith like this is *"destitute of power, inoperative it simply does not work."*

Waiting on God should never stop the flow of action in our lives. Stop using *"waiting on God"* as an excuse for inaction, complacency, and disobedience.

The walls of Jericho fell. The city was destroyed. But the promise made to Rahab and her family was fulfilled **(Joshua 6:22 NLT)**.

Her obedient faith saved her entire household.

The **Unseen** proved greater than the seen.

Chapter 5: David

Goliath was the champion of the Philistine army. He was literally a giant, standing over nine feet tall, as described in **1 Samuel 17:4(NLT):** *"Then Goliath, a Philistine champion from Gath, came out of the Philistine ranks to face the forces of Israel. He was over nine feet tall!"*

If we were only dealing with what is seen, this giant would appear unbeatable and that was exactly how the entire Israelite army viewed Goliath unstoppable and undefeatable. However, when we focus solely on the seemingly "giant" before us, we fight **for** victory instead of **from** victory. Special faith is required to conquer such an opponent. At only 17 years old, David already possessed this kind of faith the kind that could change his destiny and save his entire family.

Goliath's armor alone likely weighed as much as David himself did, if not more. Yet, that did not deter him. He knew that with God, victory was already his. When you carry faith like this, many will try to dissuade you from walking in it. That was the case for David.

King Saul considered it **ridiculous** for a young shepherd boy to challenge a seasoned warrior.

Ridiculous is a word often spoken from doubt and unbelief. *"Don't be ridiculous, David, you can't fight a giant and win."* The same spirit of doubt followed Jesus throughout His ministry: *"Don't be ridiculous, Jesus, you can't turn water into wine. Don't be ridiculous, Jesus, you can't raise someone from the dead."*

King Saul reinforced this doubt by reminding David that he was *"just a boy."* The phrases *"you're just…"* and *"don't be ridiculous"* always seem to go hand in hand. Whether Saul realized it or not, David was destined to be king. Meanwhile, Goliath had already been taunting the Israelite army for forty days, and no one had demonstrated the faith to stand up to him. How humiliating for Saul that the only one willing to face the challenge was a teenager.

Pride rose up in Saul instead of faith. There are many instances in Scripture where people of faith are discouraged from pursuing the call God has placed on their lives. Even Jesus faced opposition not just from Jewish leaders but from His own disciples. In **Matthew 16:23(NLT)**, Jesus rebuked Peter for focusing only on what was visible rather than trusting in the **Unseen**. Jesus spoke directly to the satanic influence behind Peter's words. Peter, reacting out of emotion, could not grasp the necessity of Jesus' death and resurrection. Nevertheless, Jesus knew the **Unseen** was greater than the seen, and He wanted His disciples to also understand this truth.

David's faith in God was so strong that he questioned why no one in Israel's army had already challenged Goliath. **1 Samuel 17:26(NLT)** records his words: *"David asked the soldiers standing nearby, "What will a man get for killing this Philistine and ending his defiance of Israel? Who is this pagan Philistine anyway, that he is allowed to defy the armies of the living God?"*

He could not comprehend why his people feared the giant more than they feared their God. His eyes were not fixed on the physical enemy but on the Almighty, the true Giant who created the heavens and the earth. David knew that nothing was impossible for God.

Just like David, we are called to keep our eyes on the **Unseen** rather than the seen. **Matthew 24:35(NLT)** reminds us: *"Heaven and earth will disappear, but my words will never disappear."* This is the mindset we must adopt in these last days as we stand for the salvation of our families and friends. Like David, we must move forward without fear, knowing that victory has already been secured by our God.

When we step forward in faith, the complacency of others is exposed. This was evident in David's encounter with his older brother, Eliab. In **1 Samuel**

17:28(NLT), Eliab questioned David's motives and attempted to remind him of his lowly status as a shepherd. What Eliab failed to realize was that his younger brother was more than a shepherd he was a king anointed by God. He was the only one willing to stand against the giant, and his boldness would bring salvation not only to his own family but also to all of Israel.

Similarly, when we step out in faith, others will try to remind us of our past to avoid confronting their own fear and complacency. Move forward anyway!

Faith Requires Action

Faith in God will never lead to inaction it always moves us toward action. Faith is born out of security and identity in God. David possessed both. He had already experienced God's protection in the wilderness while defending his father's sheep.

1 Samuel 17:34-35(NLT) tells us that David would chase down lions and bears when they attacked, striking them to rescue the sheep from their mouths. That was his faith in action.

This same faith emboldened him to declare victory over Goliath even before the battle began **(1Samuel 17:46 NLT).** In contrast, Goliath spoke words of doubt, using *"if"* statements in **1 Samuel 17:9(NLT):**

"If he kills me, then we will be your slaves. But if I kill him, you will be our slaves!"

David, however, spoke only words of faith. Both men moved into battle, but only one moved in belief. Goliath placed his trust in what was seen, while David's faith rested in the **Unseen**. **Deuteronomy 20:4(NLT)** reassures us of this same truth: *"For the LORD your God is going with you! He will fight for you against your enemies, and he will give you victory!"*

One Faith-Filled Stone

When the battle finally commenced, all it took was one faith-filled stone to take down the nine-foot giant. The enemy was publicly shamed, and the Philistines became subject to Israel. David's faith ignited boldness in the entire Israelite army, empowering them to chase down and defeat the remaining Philistines.

When we put our faith in the **Unseen**, we will witness the powers of the visible world crumble before us. Just as David felled Goliath with a single stone, so too can we conquer our own giants through faith in the One who has already won the victory.

Chapter 6: Esther

Esther was a Jewish woman presented before King Xerxes as a potential new wife in the Old Testament. Many young women were brought before the king at this time, but the Lord's favor rested upon Esther. By the instruction of her uncle Mordecai, she kept her Jewish heritage a secret.

The preparation process for these potential brides lasted one full year. When Esther was finally presented before the king, **the Bible says that he loved her more than any other woman and immediately crowned her as his new queen**. God had set her apart for the good works He had predestined for her. As **Ephesians 2:10(NLT)** reminds us:

"For we are God's masterpiece. He has created us anew in Christ Jesus, so we can do the good things he planned for us long ago."

Even as queen, Esther continued to conceal her Jewish identity.

Haman's Plot against the Jews

During this time, King Xerxes promoted a man named Haman, elevating him above all other officials in the empire. His authority was so great that all the king's officials were required to bow before him. However, Mordecai refused.

This act of defiance enraged Haman. When he discovered that Mordecai was a Jew, he sought not only to destroy him but also to eradicate the entire Jewish people within the empire. Haman's pride was so consuming that when he was not honored in the way he demanded, it manifested as uncontrollable rage.

True honor is never demanded, it is the harvest of a life spent sowing seeds of honor. You cannot expect a harvest if you have never planted the seeds.

Driven by hatred, Haman approached the king with a grave accusation, even offering monetary compensation to secure his request. He told King Xerxes of a certain people who disregarded the king's laws, subtly implying they were a threat to his rule. He then urged the king to issue a decree for their destruction. Trusting Haman, the king agreed without question. He granted him full authority over the lives and wealth of the Jewish people. What Xerxes did not realize was that he had just authorized the death of his own queen and her entire nationality.

The decree stated that all Jews young and old must be killed, slaughtered, and annihilated in a single day **(Esther 3:13 NLT)**.

Mordecai's Plea to Esther

At first, Queen Esther was unaware of this decree. However, she soon noticed that Mordecai was mourning publicly in sackcloth and ashes. Concerned, she sent her attendant, Hathach, to find out why.

Mordecai informed Hathach of the decree and sent him back to Esther with proof. He instructed her to go before the king and beg for mercy on behalf of her people.

Esther knew that approaching the king without an invitation was a serious offense, punishable by death unless the king extended his scepter in approval. She hesitated, knowing the risk she faced. Nevertheless, Mordecai was firm he reminded her that silence would not save her. The decree meant death for all Jews, including her.

Esther 4:14(NLT) records Mordecai's powerful words: *"If you keep quiet at a time like this, deliverance and relief for the Jews will arise from some other place, but you and your relatives will die.*

Who knows if perhaps you were made queen for just such a time as this?"

Mordecai was stirring her faith in the Unseen, urging her to overcome her fear of the seen. Risking her life in obedience to God was the only way to bring salvation not just for herself, but also for the entire Jewish people.

Faith and Obedience

Obedient faith always produces supernatural results. Let us take a moment to reflect on our own lives. Were we also born for such a time as this like Esther?

Who besides ourselves will benefit from our faith in the **Unseen**?

God has a plan for each of His children, but He will never force it upon us. He is a gentleman. He invites us to participate in something greater than ourselves, but to walk in His plan; we must be willing to step beyond what is visible.

Esther faced this choice. Through Mordecai, God was extending an invitation to be part of His plan to rescue His people from destruction. If she could push past her fear of the seen, she would step into the powerful realm of the **Unseen**.

That is exactly what she did.

Esther's Bold Move

Esther approached the king's inner court uninvited fully aware of the possible consequences. Once again, she received the favor of the Lord. The king extended his golden scepter, sparing her life and welcoming her into his presence.

Then, he asked her what she desired, offering her **anything she wished even up to half of his kingdom**.

When we move in faith in the **Unseen** rather than fear of the seen, we will experience **God's favor upon us**.

Rather than immediately exposing Haman, Esther followed **God's supernatural strategy**. She invited the king and Haman to a royal banquet. Haman, blinded by arrogance, assumed that this invitation was in his honor. He eagerly accepted and returned home to boast about it to his wife and friends.

Meanwhile, they conspired together; deciding to build a **massive pole** to impale Mordecai upon and Haman would request the king's permission to do so the following morning.

A Divine Reversal

That very night, the king was unable to sleep. He ordered that the records of his reign be read to him. As he listened, he was reminded of a time when Mordecai had **exposed a plot to assassinate him**. Curious, he asked if Mordecai had ever been honored for his loyalty. His attendants informed him that nothing had been done.

At that moment, Haman entered the court to ask for Mordecai's execution. **(Talk about bad timing!)** Before Haman could speak, the king asked him:

Esther 6:6(NKJV) *"What should be done for the man the king delights to honor?"*

Haman, assuming the king was speaking about him, eagerly described an elaborate display of royal honor. He suggested dressing the man in royal robes, placing him on the king's own horse, and having a noble official parade him through the city, shouting praises.

The king agreed to every suggestion **then commanded Haman to carry them out for Mordecai**.

Imagine the humiliation he must have felt.

Haman's Downfall

At the next banquet, the king once again asked Esther what she desired. This time, she revealed her request:

Esther 7:3(NLT) *"Spare my life and the lives of my people."*

For the first time, King Xerxes learned that his queen was a Jew and that the people Haman sought to destroy were her people.

Haman was **stunned**. This was likely the first time he realized that Esther was Jewish.

The king, enraged, demanded to know who would dare to do such a thing. Esther pointed directly at **Haman**.

As **Psalm 94:23(NLT)** declares, *"God will turn the sins of evil people back on them. He will destroy them for their sins. The LORD our God will destroy them."*

Haman's wicked plan **immediately** backfired. The king ordered that **he be impaled on the very pole he had built for Mordecai**.

Not only did Mordecai escape death, but was also promoted to **Haman's high position** and given control over his entire property. A second decree was issued, granting the Jewish people the right to **defend themselves**. With the full backing of the king, they **overpowered their enemies**.

Haman lost his life, his wealth, his position, and even his ten sons all **impaled on the very pole he had prepared for Mordecai**.

Final Thought: Be an Esther, Not a Haman

Our obedience or disobedience, has **generational consequences**.

Haman's life proves that.

Don't be a Haman! **Be an Esther**. Choose faith over fear, the **Unseen over the** seen.

Esther's story is a **timeless example** of how faith in the **Unseen** can save **not only your family but also an entire generation**.

Chapter 7: Moses

Moses was born to a Levite couple in Egypt during a time when Pharaoh had issued an order to kill all newborn Hebrew boys. His parents managed to keep him hidden for three months, but when it became impossible to conceal him any longer, they made the difficult decision to place him in a basket and send him down the river. This was an act of great sacrifice they chose his safety over their presence in his life.

What an extraordinary example of the **Unseen** being greater than the seen. Even though their situation seemed hopeless, the plan they received from the Lord ultimately saved Moses' life. Pharaoh's own daughter found him and took him in, proving that we can never go wrong when we follow God's plan.

When Moses was old enough to be weaned from his biological mother, he was returned to the princess and raised as her son. During this time, the Israelites had become enslaved by the Egyptians, and Moses grew up witnessing the suffering of his own people. This injustice never sat well with him. One day, his anger boiled over, and he killed an Egyptian who was beating an Israelite slave. This impulsive act not only made Pharaoh seek his life, but it also caused his own people to distrust him.

As a consequence of his uncontrolled anger, Moses was forced to flee Egypt. While in hiding, he came to the rescue of seven daughters of a Midian priest who were being harassed by shepherds. This act of valor earned him the favor of their father, who gave Moses his daughter in marriage. In time, they had a son named Gershom.

Meanwhile, the Israelites continued to suffer in bondage, and their cries reached the ears of the Lord. God was ready to act, but He needed someone to be His voice, hands, and feet. He chose Moses.

However, Moses responded to God out of fear, fear of the seen. The **spirit of fear** will always keep us from tapping into the unlimited power of the **Unseen**. If we cannot see past what is visible, we cannot walk in faith. Moses knew Pharaoh wanted him dead, and now the Lord was commanding him to return. Just like Moses, when our focus is on the seen, we will resist the call of the **Unseen**. We have all done it at some point in our lives.

Moses received his divine calling from a bush that was on fire but was not consumed. Yet, even this miraculous sight was not enough to stop his protests. Despite his reluctance, God was determined to use him to set His people free. To reassure Moses, the Lord even revealed His true name: **I AM**. This name was not disclosed to just anyone.

God continued to unveil His divine plan, including this astonishing promise from **Exodus 12:36(NLT):** *"The LORD caused the Egyptians to look favorably on the Israelites, and they gave the Israelites whatever they asked for. So they stripped the Egyptians of their wealth!"*

I can only imagine what went through Moses' mind when he heard that the very people who enslaved the Israelites would willingly give them their wealth. This aligns with **Proverbs 13:22(NKJV):** *"A good man leaves an inheritance to his children's children, but the wealth of the sinner is stored up for the righteous."*

Yet, despite these assurances, Moses continued to protest. The Lord demonstrated His power through mighty miracles using only a staff, but Moses remained hesitant, focusing on his limitations rather than on God's **Unseen** power. How often do we do the same, saying, *"Oh, I could never do that,"* or *"That's impossible"?*

God, in His mercy, addressed Moses' fears by appointing his brother Aaron as his spokesperson. Finally, Moses accepted his calling. At the time, Moses was 80 years old, and Aaron was 83 proving that age is no excuse for making the seen greater than the **Unseen.**

Moses and Aaron shared God's plan with the Israelites, and at first, they received favor.

However, when Pharaoh retaliated by increasing their workload, the people quickly turned against their new leaders. The Israelites were a perfect picture of those who walk in the seen rather than the **Unseen**.

They could not see beyond their suffering. How often do we do the same? We allow our trauma and circumstances to dictate our faith instead of believing in what God has promised.

The Lord's plan to free His people would not be thwarted by the seen. He instructed Moses to return to Pharaoh, warning him of plagues to come if he refused to release the Israelites. Pharaoh's heart remained hardened, despite experiencing one plague after another. There were moments when he seemed to soften, only to change his mind once the plague ceased. Many believers act the same way crying out to God in desperation but quickly forgetting Him once they receive their breakthrough.

Moses and Aaron remained steadfast in faith, knowing that freedom was coming. This mirrors the prayers of those of us interceding for our loved ones to be delivered from the bondage of sin. The seen tries to deceive us into thinking our prayers are ineffective, but those who understand the **Unseen** know that God is always at work.

Isaiah 55:8(NLT) says, *"My thoughts are nothing like your thoughts," says the LORD. "And my ways are far beyond anything you could imagine."*

The Lord sent ten plagues upon Egypt, many of which only affected the Egyptians, displaying His favor over Israel. Pharaoh's power seemed insurmountable, having enslaved an entire nation for over hundreds of years. Yet the story of Moses proves that what we **cannot see** is greater than what we **do see**. Despite Pharaoh's plans, God's plan was greater.

The final plague broke Pharaoh's resistance the death of every firstborn in Egypt, including his own son. This devastation forced him to release the Israelites. Not only were they freed, but God also caused the Egyptians to **favor** them, giving them their wealth an undeniable fulfillment of **Ephesians 3:20(NIV)**: *"Now to Him who is able to do immeasurably more than all we ask or imagine..."*

When we allow our past trauma to harden our hearts, we can become blind to the **Unseen** power of God. Pharaoh's hardened heart cost him dearly not just his son, but his army, his legacy, and ultimately his life.

Moses, on the other hand, moved forward in **faith**. Even when circumstances looked impossible, he trusted in God's plan. **Numbers 23:19(NLT)** reassures us: *"God is not a man, so He does not lie. He is not human, so He does not change His mind. Has He ever spoken and failed to act? Has He ever promised and not carried it through?"*

When the Israelites found themselves trapped between Pharaoh's army and the Red Sea, panic set in. But the Lord reminded Moses that He had already given him the power to part the waters. As Moses lifted his staff, the sea miraculously divided, and the Israelites walked through on dry ground.

The **Unseen** had once again prepared a way for the seen.

Did the Israelites recognize God's hand upon them before this miraculous moment? No. They panicked and complained, yet God's grace still covered them. Even in our unfaithfulness, He remains faithful.

2 Timothy 2:13(NLT) *"If we are unfaithful, He remains faithful, for He cannot deny who He is."*

We will always miss the mark when we allow the seen to be greater than the **Unseen**.

Moses' obedience led to one of the greatest miracles recorded in the Bible a story that has fueled the faith of believers for generations. His faith in the **Unseen** didn't just save his family it saved an entire nation. What will your faith in the **Unseen** accomplish?

Chapter 8: Jesus

"For this is how God loved the world: He gave His one and only Son, so that everyone who believes in Him will not perish but have eternal life. God sent His own Son into the world not to judge the world, but to save the world through Him!" **John 3:16-17 NLT)**

Through one man (Adam), all of creation was condemned, but through another man, all of creation was redeemed. That man is Jesus. His sole purpose, according to the Bible, was to come as a sacrifice for all. When I say all, I literally mean all!

1 John 2:2(MSG) states, *"When He served as a sacrifice for our sins, He solved the sin problem for good not only ours but the whole world's."*

Faith in the **Unseen** transaction of our sinful lives for His sinless life was His purpose, plan, and desire.

1 Corinthians 5:21(NLT) affirms, *"For God made Christ, who never sinned, to be the offering for our sin, so that we could be made right with God through Christ."*

The execution of this plan was not only perfect with eternal rewards it was also so powerful that it shook the entire earth, tearing the veil of the Holy of Holies and bridging the gap between all of humanity and the One who created it. Jesus was the sacrifice that bridged that gap.

1 Timothy 2:5(NLT) confirms, *"There is one God and one Mediator who can reconcile God and humanity the man Christ Jesus."*

Faith in Jesus alone is the faith that can save our families. He is the **Unseen** power that is greater than the seen. Salvation is found through faith and belief in who Jesus is, what He has done for us, and a heart of repentance.

Acts 3:19(NLT) calls us to action: *"Now repent of your sins and turn to God, so that your sins may be wiped away."* The testimony of our salvation directly affects the salvation of those around us. If you have not yet given your life to Jesus, there is no time to waste. The Bible says that today is the day of salvation.

2 Corinthians 6:2(NLT) reminds us, *"At just the right time, I heard you. On the day of salvation, I helped you." Indeed, the "right time" is now. Today is the day of salvation."*

Jesus came the first time in mercy and grace to sacrifice His life for all humanity. However, the next time He comes, it will be with judgment. He clearly states in **John 3:16** that His heart is that **no one** perishes but that **all** should have eternal life. His heart is to come back to earth and take all humanity to heaven with Him. Unfortunately, the reality is that some will refuse His free eternal gift and instead face His judgment.

Do not be one who faces His judgment! Be one who accepts this miraculous gift and eagerly awaits the second coming of Jesus.

Philippians 3:20(NLT) declares, *"But we are citizens of heaven, where the Lord Jesus Christ lives. And we are eagerly waiting for Him to return as our Savior."*

If you are ready to make this eternal decision today, simply say this prayer, believe it in your heart, and confess it aloud with your mouth:

"Jesus, I repent of my sins, I ask You to come into my heart and change me from the inside out. I surrender my finite life and receive Your eternal life. In Jesus' name, Amen."

Romans 10:9(NKJV) says, *"that if you confess with your mouth the Lord Jesus and believe in your heart that God has raised Him from the dead, you will be saved."*

One thing that the people mentioned above all had in common is that they did not let others' views of what they thought they should be change who they knew God had called them to be. They did not have cookie-cutter faith; their faith was unique to their calling, their gifting's, and their supernatural destinies.

- **Abraham** knew he was destined to be the father of many nations despite what it looked like in the natural. Many likely tried to get him to see a different picture for his life as he waited decades on the Lord for his promised son. He chose to stay in faith, knowing that God would be faithful to His word.
- **Noah's** obedience saved his family despite how everyone looked at him while he was building a huge ark during a time when it had never rained before.
- **Joseph** knew his destiny was to rule despite the way his brothers and parents saw him. He was more than a younger brother, more than a slave, and more than a prisoner.
- **Rahab** knew her family would be saved if she hid the Lord's spies and obeyed them, despite the way those in the world around her viewed her.
- **David** knew he was destined to be king despite the way his brothers, his father, and King Saul saw him.

- **Esther** knew she was born for that moment despite the threat to her life and the lives of her people. She could have settled into her position as Queen, but she knew she was meant for more than that.
- **Moses** knew he was meant to free the Israelites from slavery despite a fear of speaking, despite how the Israelites saw him, and despite the hardened heart of Pharaoh.
- **Jesus** knew why He came to earth, and no one was able to change the course of His life! Through hatred, jealousy, betrayal, and even early attempts on His life, He stayed faithful to the Father's plan for Him. We are to continue His ministry! We are to be extensions of His ministry.

Like all those who have gone before us, we must remain faithful to the Unseen.

Hebrews 12:1(NLT) reminds us: *"Therefore, since we are surrounded by such a huge crowd of witnesses to the life of faith, let us strip off every weight that slows us down, especially the sin that so easily trips us up. And let us run with endurance the race God has set before us."*

We are to stay faithful to the Father's plan for our lives, not man's.

Proverbs 29:25(NLT) warns, *"Fearing people is a dangerous trap, but trusting the LORD means safety."* The only one who can understand the unique calling on our lives is us! Additionally, the only one who can prevent the unique calling on our lives from manifesting is ourselves.

The gifting's and callings of God are irrevocable, according to **Romans 11:29**. Following man's plan for our lives is the beginning of the fear of man and the end of the fear of the Lord. Faith in man cannot and will not save our families. However, faith in the **Unseen** God can and will because He alone has the power to redeem, restore, and lead our families into lasting hope and purpose. **John 14:1(NLT)** *"Do not let your hearts be troubled. Trust in God, and trust also in Me (Jesus)."*

The **Unseen** is and will always be greater than the seen!

3 POINT TURN
PUBLISHING

FLOODED
WITH
LIGHT

**BIBLICAL REVELATIONS TO
EQUIP THE BELIEVER WALK IN
THE SUPERNATURAL**

*The power of the Holy Spirit within
the believer is what illuminates the
eyes of our heart, bringing clarity,
strength, and hope.*

**JOSHUA & MIREYA
TUFANO**
Author

ORDER NOW 🌐 3pointturn.org

3 POINT TURN Ministries

FOLLOW US ON
All Podcast Platforms

@3.pointturn
@mireya.tufano
@tufanovich

@3.pointturn
@mireya.tufano
@tufanovich

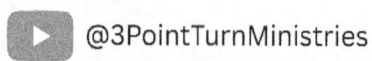
@3PointTurnMinistries

TUNE IN WEEKLY FOR UPLIFTING CONTENT!